KU-115-305

The Oxford Book of Italian Madrigals

Edited by Alec Harman

Oxford University Press
Music Department
37 Dover Street
London WIX 4AH

Contents

0193436477

HAMPSHIRE COUNTY LIBRARY

784 | 80 4 8 366

C014039959

Index of composers

Foreword

One of the principal differences between late Renaissance secular part-music[1] in Italy and in England lies in the far greater amount produced in the former country. This was partly due to the fact that in Italy compared to England the period in question was roughly twice as long, and the number of composers (many of them foreigners from north of the Alps), even allowing for the longer period, was far greater, as was the general productivity of each composer. Thus, while there were 23 English composers who produced at least one book containing secular part-music (only eight published more than one book), and who produced a total of nearly 800 pieces[2], in Italy there were close to 600 such composers, the great majority of whom wrote at least two books (some composers were especially productive, e.g. Monte with 36 books, Marenzio with 23, Wert with 16). The total can only be guessed at from the fact that the number of madrigals alone produced by the leading composers of the genre – Festa, Verdelot, Arcadelt, Willaert, Rore, Palestrina, Lassus, A. Gabrieli, Monte, Wert, Marenzio, Gesualdo, and Monteverdi – is almost exactly 2,900. Of these almost 300 consist of settings of the same texts by two or more of the above composers (e.g. Nos. 15, 20, and 42 in this anthology), another striking difference between the madrigal in Italy and England, for the latter produced only 27 such comparative settings.

To make a representative selection of the best pieces from such a number is clearly extremely difficult and subjective, and it is equally clear that another editor could make a selection that was very different yet just as representative. But it is hoped that what is here presented will give a fair reflection not only of the quality of the music, but also of the most important composers, the various types of secular part-music, the number and kinds of voices used, the range in mood, and the development of the madrigal – by far the most important secular type.

Generally speaking, the madrigal began as a sentimental, amorous piece for usually four voices, displaying a rather casual concern for matching the music either to the accents of a poem or to its more evocative words or phrases. The lack of careful accentuation may have been because the great majority of the early madrigalists were foreigners, but it was a foreigner, Willaert, who first stressed the importance of accurate text-setting. Attempts to portray in the music the meaning of certain words or phrases (word- or mood-painting) became a significant feature of the madrigal around 1550, and developed thereafter; it included such devices as 'wavy' vocal lines to denote 'sea' or 'flight', white and black semibreves to the words 'day' and 'night' respectively, triple metre when dancing was mentioned, and semitonal rises and falls or chromatic chords to express anguish. Moreover,

1. In this Foreword a distinction is made between secular part-music, which covers all types, and the madrigal itself, but in the title, as in the companion volume of English madrigals, the term 'madrigal' includes other types, such as *balletti, canzonette*, etc., but not the 'spiritual madrigal'.
2. Here and throughout this anthology any piece that is divided into two or more sections or 'Parts' is counted as a single composition.

from *c.*1550 on not only were the accents of the text increasingly matched in the music, but also the emotional range of the poetry chosen for madrigal settings began to widen. As a result of the latter, compositional techniques expanded, in particular the use of five and, to a lesser extent, six voices instead of four, and the deliberate choice as 'time' signature, for expressive reasons, of either '₵' or 'C'; in the former the pulse was a semibreve, and the shortest note set to a syllable, the shortest harmonic movement, and the longest dissonance was usually a minim, while in the latter signature these note-values were halved. Most composers increasingly used the signature 'C', reserving '₵' for the most serious madrigals, and there was also a tendency to combine the above features in a single madrigal, with a signature of either '₵' (e.g. No.42) or 'C' (e.g. No.46), thus providing greater variety in the speed of syllabic underlay and harmonic movement and in the length of dissonance.

In order to make the original notation look more conventional, the note-values have been halved throughout this anthology, so keeping the distinction between '₵' and 'C'. Thus the original notation in '₵' (with two semibreves per bar) becomes our modern '₵' or 2/2, and while the original 'C' (sometimes transcribed with two minims to the bar) should strictly become 2/4, the bar length has been doubled in order to reduce the number of bar-lines, and so becomes 4/4 or our modern 'C'. The speed of the original semibreve and minim pulses in '₵' and 'C' respectively seem to have been the same, i.e. according to contemporary evidence, the rate of a normal heart-beat (M.M.70), but it is unlikely that this was inflexible. Hence in this book, with note-values halved, the tempo shown in square brackets at the beginning of each piece is usually within the range of minim (half-note) or crotchet (quarter-note) equalling M.M.60-80, most of the exceptions being some lighter pieces, in which the pulse is faster, and some of the madrigals which combine the features of '₵' and 'C', in which it is slower.

The growing importance of the text was fundamental to the development of the Italian madrigal, for it was increasingly the text that caused composers to decide on what mode, metre, and voices they would use for a particular madrigal, and, for a particular word or phrase, the kind of vocal line, note-values, rhythms, textual underlay, harmonies, dissonances, textures, and vocal colour. It is, therefore, essential, when performing an Italian madrigal, to understand the poem as a whole, as well as certain words and phrases that receive special musical treatment. It is equally essential to accentuate the text correctly, and this brings us to one of the most striking and basic differences between the music of the Renaissance period and earlier and that of the Baroque period and later, namely, the rhythmic flexibility and irregularity of the former. Thus in Renaissance part-music each voice was, with very few exceptions, printed in separate part-books, as, for example, in string quartet music today; but unlike the latter there were no indications of tempo or dynamics, no expression marks, and no regularly spaced bar-lines with their implied regular accents, because accents were derived from the text or, in a melisma (i.e. several notes to a syllable), from the length of a note in its context, a longer note than those flanking it being more accented. Thus, while it is imperative for today's singers that the music be arranged in score and regularly barred, it is also imperative that singers recognize that such barring has no automatic accentual significance; in other words, in a 2/2 or 4/4 bar the first minim or the first and third crotchets respectively will not invariably be accented.

In order to assist singers to accentuate correctly, the following points, some being modifications of accepted practice, should be studied:

1. In homorhythmic passages where all or most of the voices are, in effect, in triple metre, though still governed by 'Ȼ' or 'C', the number '3' in square brackets is used to denote $\frac{3/6}{4/8}$ or $\frac{3/6}{2/4}$, depending on the context. But in certain cases, for the sake of clarity, the actual time signature (in square brackets) is given. In those rare passages where the original notation (e.g. black notes) and/or signature indicate triple metre, the number '3' is used but without square brackets, with the original signature, if different from '3', footnoted, and black notation shown thus: ⌐ ¬ above the notes. In each case the relationship between the triple metre passage and the duple metre that flanks it is given in square brackets above the stave.

2. The first minim in a bar in 'Ȼ', and the first and third crotchets in 'C', are accented, unless preceded or succeeded by a longer note (or the equivalent in shorter note-values), including tied notes, or by a note with a stress mark (-).

3. The first quaver (eighth-note) in a group of two is accented unless preceded by an accented note or a quaver rest.

4. The third quaver in a group of four is accented.

5. The first quaver in a group of three is accented unless preceded by a quaver rest or a dotted crotchet.

6. A single quaver is unaccented.

7. The stress mark is used for exceptions to, or instances not covered by, the above.

8. Generally speaking, the accent in Italian is on the penultimate syllable if the word ends in a vowel (am*ore*), and on the final syllable if the word ends with a consonant or an accented vowel (mor*ir*, pietà).

Although the madrigal was, as stated earlier, by far the most important type of secular part-music in the Renaissance, there were a number of other types. These, in general, were set for fewer voices, much lighter, not to say coarser, in tone, homophonic in texture, and strophic, and thus provided a marked contrast with the sentimental or serious, essentially polyphonic, and through-composed madrigal. Some of these types are included in this anthology, namely: *villanella* (Nos. 11, 36) – a simple strophic song, which often deliberately included musical solecisms, e.g. parallel fifths or triads. It was the most common non-madrigalian type, and incorporated a number of sub-types, among them the *mascherata* (No. 7) – sung during carnival processions by 'masked' singers advertising various local trades or professions, in this case dance instructors, and the *giustiniana* (No. 31) – a strophic song for three male voices, representing decrepit old men who stutter (a rare affliction in Italy) and whose amorous desires exceed their capabilities! *Canzonetta* (Nos. 37, 49) – literally 'little song' – sometimes 'parodied' the madrigal, as in No. 49, in which the opening of No. 23 is quoted. *Balletto* (Nos. 44, 45), a strophic 'dance' song, was strongly rhythmic, and usually had a 'Fa la' refrain.

The translations of the poems have been either done by or checked by an Italian specialist, Anna Bartrum, except for those by H. E. Smither and A. Illiano in A. Einstein's *The Italian Madrigal*, Vol. III (i.e. Nos. 2, 5, 7, 9, 11-13, 18, 26, 49, and 55), and No. 31 by Mrs Roberta Tozer, to all of whom the editor expresses his thanks. In every case an attempt has been made in the translations to match the original position of an Italian word in a poetic line, so that the singer can see when and how certain words are 'painted' in the music; the result may at times be somewhat convoluted, and for this the editor is wholly responsible.

The original clefs and signatures, and the initial note in each voice, are placed at the beginning of each piece. The seven clefs in common use in the Renaissance have been reduced to three; thus the G clef is used for the original G clef as well as the soprano and mezzo-soprano C clefs, the octave-transposed G clef is used for the original tenor C clef, and the F clef is used for the original bass and baritone F clefs. This leaves the alto C clef, the only one common to the two basic clef combinations in the Renaissance, namely: treble, mezzo-soprano, alto, baritone, and soprano, alto, tenor, bass (in pieces for more than four voices any clef could be doubled). In the former combination the alto clef is replaced in this book by the octave-transposed G clef, and in the latter by the G clef.

A number of the pieces have been transposed up or down a whole tone in order that, in general, the highest note of the soprano and tenor does not go above g'' and g' respectively, or the alto below g. In this connection it should be mentioned that during the Renaissance there was no fixed pitch, and hence what was written in, say, the Ionian mode (our C major) could have sounded in B flat or D major. This applies equally to instruments, and instrumental participation in the vocal music of the period (i.e. the doubling or replacing of a vocal line by a suitable instrument) was part of performance practice. It is probable, however, that those pieces in which the music is very closely wedded to the text as regards expression were ideally performed by unaccompanied voices. Ornamentation of the written note was also a part of performance practice, but it is recommended that any embellishments should be simple, and restricted to the principal cadences and to the repeat of a musical phrase or passage[1]. (For further information, H. M. Brown's admirable little book *Embellishing Sixteenth-Century Music* should be consulted). Such improvisation can only be done by one singer per part, and implies a small group of not more than three singers per part, a number supported by the little evidence that has survived. This is vocal chamber music, not choral music, and hence clarity of sound is all-important; in other words, undue vibrato in any voice will mar the chordal purity of the ensemble.

As noted earlier, there are no expression or dynamic marks in the original prints or manuscripts, and yet it is unthinkable that no sense of mood or structure was conveyed by the singers of that time; thus it is reasonable to assume that the text determined the dynamic levels and gradations and the 'colour' of the voices, that in a passage where a motif is shared between all or most of the voices, the voice with the motif should stand out, that the rise or fall of a vocal line should also affect, naturally, dynamic gradations, and that ritardandos should accompany final cadences, but that everything should be done modestly, avoiding extremes.

The pieces in this anthology have been arranged chronologically. Those that are not madrigals are indicated by their precise type being given in parentheses in the list of Contents, which also includes the date of the first known print of each piece and its vocal scoring. The original spelling of the poems has been retained, except for the deletion of 'h' and the addition or omission of some accents and apostrophes, mostly according to modern usage; much of the punctuation is also editorial. Where known, the name of the author of a poem is placed opposite that of the composer of a piece. Errors in the texts and music are footnoted and placed at the bottom of the page on which they occur, and editorial accidentals are printed small. The music is followed by a list which gives the short title of the first known print of each piece, and in parentheses, if it differs, the source used by the editor.

ALEC HARMAN

1. Except in Nos. 7, 11, 31, 36, 37, 44, 45, and 49, double-bars and repeat dots are editorial, passages being written out in full in the original.

1
DORMEND' UN GIORNO

VERDELOT

© Oxford University Press 1983

Printed in Great Britain

Photocopying this copyright material is **ILLEGAL**

2
AMOR MI FA MORIRE

B. Dragonetto

WILLAERT

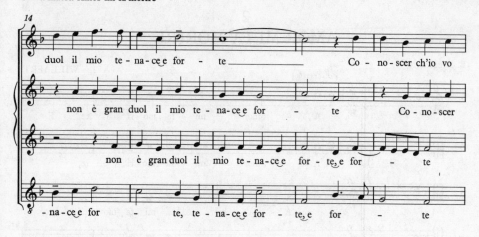

3
ITALIA MIA

Petrarch

VERDELOT

4
QUANTO PIÙ M'ARDE

WILLAERT

5
COSÌ SUAV' È'L FOCO

FESTA

6
IL BIANCO E DOLCE CIGNO

A. d'Avalos

ARCADELT

7

CHI LA GAGLIARDA, DONNA, VO IMPARARE

DA NOLA

① ♩ (= ♪) in original in all parts.

si - mo_ma - stri fi - ni,_ ma - stri fi - ni,_ ma - stri   fi - ni,
vol - te_che sa - li - mo,_ che sa - li - mo,_che sa - li - mo,   Che   de
el - le bi - so - gnia sta - re, bi - so - gnia sta - re, bi - so - gnia   sta - re,
no - me_Mar - ti - no,_ Mar - ti - no,_Mar - ti - no,

si - mo_ ma - stri fi - ni,_ ma - stri fi - ni, _ ma - stri   fi - ni,
vol - te_che sa - li - mo,_ che sa - li - mo,_che sa - li - mo,   Che ___ de ser' e
el - le bi - so - gnia sta - re, bi - so - gnia sta - re, bi - so - gnia   sta - re,
no - me_Mar - ti - no,_ Mar - ti - no,_Mar - ti - no,

si - mo_ ma - stri fi - ni,_ ma - stri fi - ni,_ ma - stri   fi - ni,
vol - te_che sa - li - mo,_ che sa - li - mo,_che sa - li - mo,   Che ___ de ser' e
el - le bi - so - gnia sta - re, bi - so - gnia sta - re, bi - so - gnia   sta - re,
no - me_Mar - ti - no,_ Mar - ti - no,_Mar - ti - no,

ser' e de ma - ti - na Mai man - chia - mo, mai man - chia - mo di so - na - - -
de ma - ti - na Mai man - chia - mo, mai man - chia - mo ___ di   so - na - -
de ma - ti - na Mai man - chia - mo, mai man - chia - mo, mai man - chia - mo di   so - na - -

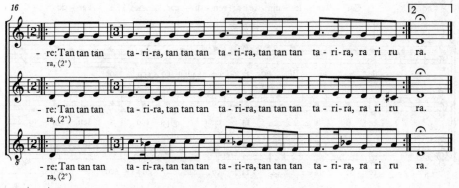

- re: Tan tan tan   ta - ri - ra, tan tan tan   ta - ri - ra, tan tan tan   ta - ri - ra, ra ri ru   ra.
ra, (2°)

- re: Tan tan tan   ta - ri - ra, tan tan tan   ta - ri - ra, tan tan tan   ta - ri - ra, ra ri ru   ra.
ra, (2°)

- re: Tan tan tan   ta - ri - ra, tan tan tan   ta - ri - ra, tan tan tan   ta - ri - ra, ra ri ru   ra.
ra, (2°)

② ♩ (= ♪) in original in all parts, here and elsewhere.

8

DORMENDO UN GIORNO

ARCADELT

cal - do   du - ra,   sempr' il   cal - do   du - ra

cal - do   du - ra, sempr'   il   cal - do   du -   -   -

cal - do   du - ra, sempr'   il   cal - do   du -   -   -

Che   la   fiam - ma   d'a -   mor a - cqua non

-    -   - ra Che la fiam - ma   d'a - mor a - cqua

-    -   - ra Che la fiam - ma   d'a -   mor a - cqua

cu -   -   -   -   - ra, che la fiam - ma   d'a -

non   cu -   -   -   ra, che la fiam - ma   d'a -

non   cu -   -   ra, che la fiam - ma   d'a -

- mor a - cqua non   cu -   -   -   - ra.

- mor a - cqua   non   cu -   -   - ra.

- mor a - cqua   non cu -   - ra.

9
IO MI SON GIOVINETTA

Boccaccio

D. M. FERRABOSCO

10
STRANE RUPPI

N. Amanio

RORE

11
TUTTE LE VECCHIE SON MALECIOSE

DI MAIO

12
QUEST' IO TESSEVA E QUELLE

CORTECCIA

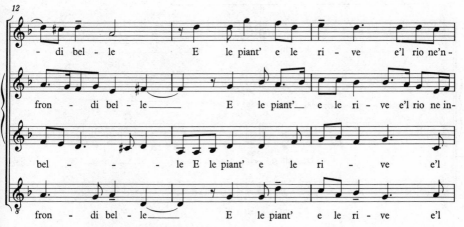

13
ANCOR CHE COL PARTIRE

14
INGIUSTISSIMO AMOR

Ariosto

FESTA

S. In - giu-stis - si - mo A - mor, in - giu-stis - si - mo A -

A. In - giu-stis - si - mo A - mor, in - giu-stis - si - mo A -

T. In - giu-stis - si - mo A - mor, in - giu-stis - si - mo A -

-mor, per - chè sì ra - ro, per-chè sì ra - ro Cor -

-mor, per - chè sì ra - ro, per-chè sì ra - -

-mor, per - chè sì ra - ro, sì ra - ro Cor -

- ri - spon - den - ti fai no - stri de - si - - - -

- ro Cor - ri - spon - den - ti fai no - stri de - - -

- ri - spon - den - ti fai no - stri de - si - ri, no - stri de -

- - - - ri? On - de, per - fid', ad - vien che t'è sì

- si - ri? On - de, per - fid', ad - vien che t'è sì ca - - -

- si - ri? On - de, per - fid', ad - vien che t'è sì

15
MIA BENIGNA FORTUNA

Petrarch

LASSUS

16
CANTAI, OR PIANGO

Petrarch

LASSUS

17
O MORTE, ETERNO FIN

G. B. G. Cinzio (?)   RORE

18
O SONNO

G. Della Casa

RORE

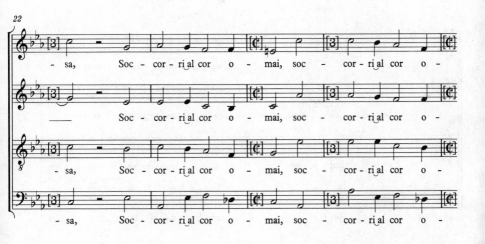

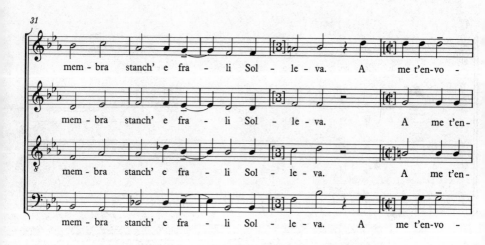

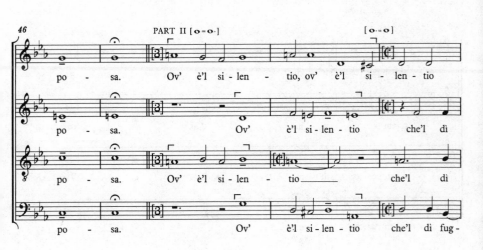

19
L'ALTO SIGNOR

Petrarch

RORE

*S.2 and Alto exchange parts in the repeat.

20
MIA BENIGNA FORTUNA

Petrarch

RORE

vi-ta in pian - to, E i gior-ni o -
-nar tut - ta mia vi-ta in pian - to, E i gior-ni o -
me - nar tut - ta mia vi-ta in pian - to, E i gior-ni o -
-nar tut - ta mia vi - ta in pian - to, E i gior-ni o -

- scu - ri e le do - glio - se not - - ti;
- scu - ri e i gior-ni o-scu - ri e le do - glio - se not -
- scu - ri e le do - glio - se not - ti;
- scu - ri e le do - glio - se

I miei gra - vi so - spir non van-no in ri - -
- - ti; I miei gra - vi so - spir non van-no in ri - -
I miei gra - vi so - spir non van-no in ri - -
not - ti; I miei gra - vi so - spir non van-no in ri -

21
CHI SALIRÀ PER ME

Ariosto

WERT

22
CANTAI, OR PIANGO

Petrarch

WILLAERT

non men di dol - cez - za___ del pian - ger pren - do,

- cez - za del pian-ger pren - do, che del can-to pre - si, che___

non men di dol - cez - za del pian-ger pren - do, che del can-to pre -

pian-ger pren - do, che del can - to pre - si, che del can - to

di dol-cez - za del pian-ger pren - do, che del can - to pre -

pren - - do, che del can - to pre - si,

che del___ can - to pre - si, Ch'a la ca-

___ del can-to pre - si, Ch'a la ca-gion, non a l'ef-fet-to‿in-te -

- si, che del can - to pre - si, Ch'a la___ ca-gion, non

pre - si, Ch'a la ca-gion, non a l'ef-fet-to‿in-te - si Son'

- si, Ch'a la ca-gion, non a l'ef-fet-to‿in-te - si Son'___

che del can - to pre - si, Ch'a la ca-gion,

23
IO SON FERITO, AHI LASSO

PALESTRINA

24
QUEST'AFFANNATO MIO DOGLIOSO CORE

RORE

25
VESTIVA I COLLI

H. Capilupi

PALESTRINA

26
DUE ROSE FRESCHE

Petrarch

A. GABRIELI

27
NE L'ARIA IN QUESTI DÌ

RORE

28
LA VER L'AURORA

PALESTRINA

29
LEGGIADRE NINFE

MONTE

*Octave above permissible

30
AHI, CHI MI ROMPE IL SONNO

D. Veniero

MONTE

31
QUANDO SARÀ MAI QUEL ZONORNO

BELL' HAVER

32
S'IO ESCA VIVO DE' DUBBIOSI SCOGLI

Petrarch

LASSUS

* Octave lower

33
CHE FA OGGI IL MIO SOLE

MARENZIO

34
GIÀ TORNA A RALLEGRAR L'ARIA E LA TERRA

MARENZIO

35
FA CH'IO RIVEGGIA

MONTE

36
FUGGIRÒ TANT', AMORE

MARENZIO

[♩ = mm 96]

S.
1. Fug - gi - rò, fug - gi - rò, fug - gi - rò tant', A - mo -
2. Fug - gi - rò, fug - gi - rò, fug - gi - rò tan - to, tan -
3. Fug - gi - rò, fug - gi - rò, fug - gi - rò il for - te lac -
4. Fug - gi - rò, fug - gi - rò, fug - gi - rò dun - que A - mo -

A.
1. Fug - gi - rò, fug - gi - rò, fug - gi - rò tant', A - mo -
2. Fug - gi - rò, fug - gi - rò, fug - gi - rò tan - to, tan -
3. Fug - gi - rò, fug - gi - rò, fug - gi - rò il for - te lac -
4. Fug - gi - rò, fug - gi - rò, fug - gi - rò dun - que A - mo -

B.
1. Fug - gi - rò, fug - gi - rò, fug - gi - rò tant', A - mo -
2. Fug - gi - rò, fug - gi - rò, fug - gi - rò tan - to, tan -
3. Fug - gi - rò, fug - gi - rò, fug - gi - rò il for - te lac -
4. Fug - gi - rò, fug - gi - rò, fug - gi - rò dun - que A - mo -

3

- re, Che sce - me - rà l'ar - do - re, Le fiamm'
- to, Che ces - se - rà il mio pian - to, Il no -
- cio, Et u - sci - rò d'im - pac - cio, Ne di
- re, Sciol - to dal fie - ro ar - do - re, E di -

- re, Che sce - me - rà l'ar - do - re, Le fiamm'
- to, Che ces - se - rà il mio pian - to, Il no -
- cio, Et u - sci - rò d'im - pac - cio, Ne di
- re, Sciol - to dal fie - ro ar - do - re, E di -

- re, Che sce - me - rà l'ar - do - re, Le fiamm'
- to, Che ces - se - rà il mio pian - to, Il no -
- cio, Et u - sci - rò d'im - pac - cio, Ne di
- re, Sciol - to dal fie - ro ar - do - re, E di -

37
MENTRE IL CUCULO IL SUO CUCU CANTAVA

CAIMO

38
VEZZOSI AUGELLI

T. Tasso

WERT

39
FORSENNATA GRIDAVA

T. Tasso

WERT

40
I' VO PIANGENDO

Petrarch

A. GABRIELI

41
TIRSI MORIR VOLEA

Guarini

A. GABRIELI

42
MIA BENIGNA FORTUNA

Petrarch   WERT

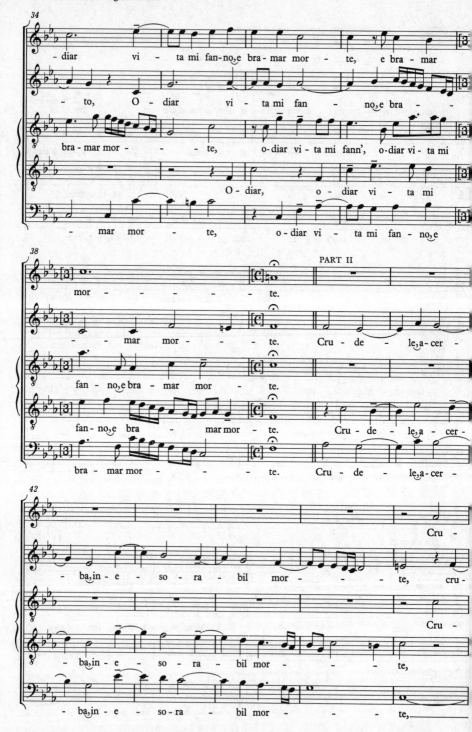

43
ECCO MORMORAR L'ONDE

MONTEVERDI

44
OVE NE VAI SÌ IN FRETTA
(Il premiato)

GASTOLDI

1. O - ve ne vai sì in fret - ta, O vi - tal del mio
2. Fra mil - le Nin - fe e - let - ta T'ha per me so - lo A -
3. O sia tu be - ne - det - ta Poi che non par - tian -
4. Go - ia com' io per - fet - ta Non pro-va al-cun Pa -

① Note values halved in this and other sections in triple metre and black notation.
② 'C' in all parts.

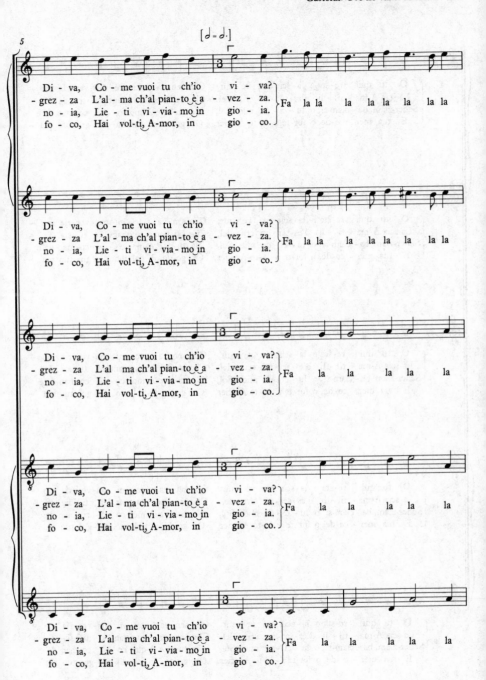

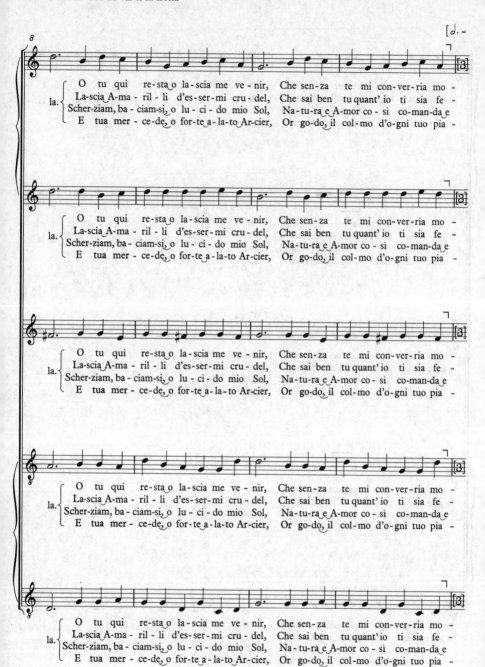

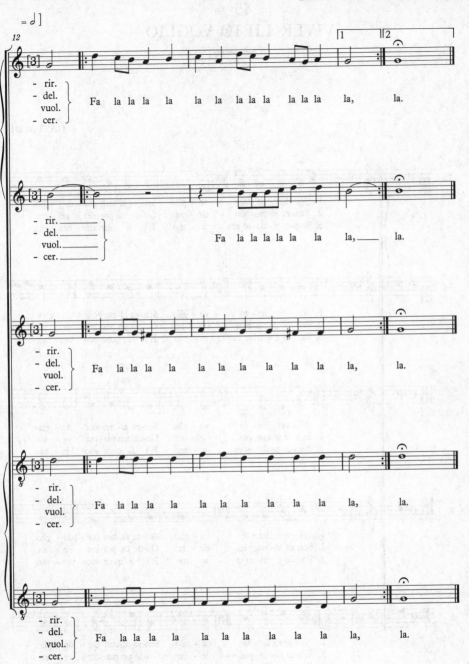

45
VIVER LIETO VOGLIO
(Il bell' umore)

GASTOLDI

S.1
1. Vi - ver lie - to vo - glio Sen-za al-cun cor - dog - lio.
2. Sen-za al-cun pen - sie - ro Go-do un pia-cer ve - ro.
3. Bac-co a-do-ro et a - mo E'l li-quor suo bra-mo.

S.2
1. Vi - ver lie - to vo - glio Sen-za al-cun cor - do - glio.
2. Sen-za al-cun pen - sie - ro Go-do un pia-cer ve - ro. La la
3. Bac-co a-do-ro et a - mo E'l li-quor suo bra-mo.

A.
1. Vi - ver lie - to vo - glio Sen-za al-cun cor - do - glio.
2. Sen-za al-cun pen - sie - ro Go-do un pia-cer ve - ro.
3. Bac-co a-do-ro et a - mo E'l li-quor suo bra-mo.

T.
1. Vi - ver lie - to vo - glio Sen-za al-cun cor - do - glio.
2. Sen-za al-cun pen - sie - ro Go-do un pia-cer ve - ro.
3. Bac-co a-do-ro et a - mo E'l li-quor suo bra-mo.

B.
1. Vi - ver lie - to vo - glio Sen-za al-cun cor - do - glio.
2. Sen-za al-cun pen - sie - ro Go-do un pia-cer ve - ro.
3. Bac-co a-do-ro et a - mo E'l li-quor suo bra-mo.

* ♩ rest

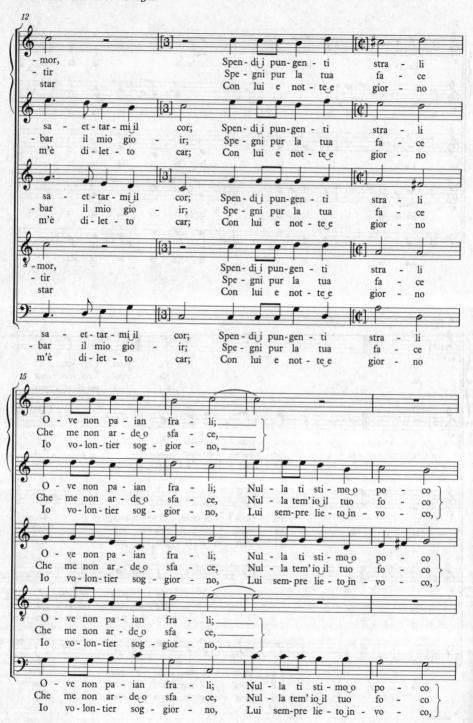

46
CRUDA AMARILLI

Guarini

MARENZIO

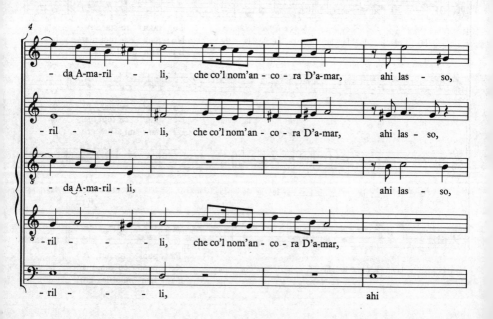

47
LANGUISCO E MORO

GESUALDO

48
LUCI SERENE E CHIARE

GESUALDO

① # (=♮) 2nd time
② ♮ (=♭) 2nd time

49
S'UDIA UN PASTOR L'ALTR' HIERI

VECCHI

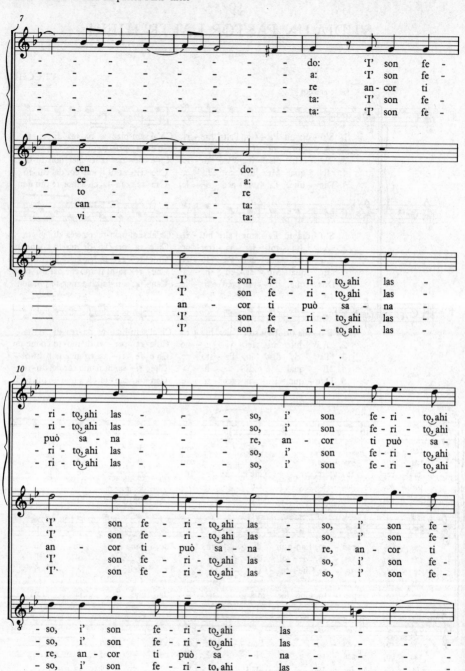

50
SOLO E PENSOSO

Petrarch

MARENZIO

*G [= F]

51
SI CH'IO VORREI MORIRE

MONTEVERDI

* C♯ = D♯

52
AH DOLENTE PARTITA

Guarini

MONTEVERDI

53
QUEL AUGELLIN CHE CANTA

Guarini

MONTEVERDI

*Next five notes an octave lower

54
RESTA DI DARMI NOIA

GESUALDO

Re - sta di dar - mi no - ia, re - sta

di dar - mi no - ia, Pen - sier cru - do e fal - la -

55
ITENE MIE QUERELE

LUZZASCHI

I - te-ne mie que - re - le Pre - ci - pi - to-se a vo - - -

I - te-ne mie que - re - le Pre - ci - pi - to-se a vo -

I - te-ne mie que - re - le Pre-ci-pi-to-se a vo -

I - te-ne mie que - re - le

I - te-ne mie que - re - le Pre -

- lo, a vo - - lo A lei, a lei che m'è ca-

- lo, a vo - - lo A lei, a lei che m'è ca-

- lo, a vo - - lo, a vo - lo A lei, a lei che m'è ca-

Pre - ci - pi - to-se a vo - - lo A lei, a lei che m'è ca-

- ci - pi - to-se a vo - - lo A lei che m'è ca-

Sources

1. First book of madrigals *a*5. *c*.1535. (Verdelot – *Le dotte, et eccellente compositioni . . . c*.1538).
2. Verdelot – Second book of madrigals *a*4. 1536.
3. Second book of madrigals *a*5. 1538. (As No. 1).
4. Verdelot – *Le dotte, et eccellente compositioni . . . c*.1538.
5. Arcadelt – Fourth book of madrigals *a*4. 1539.
6. First book of madrigals *a*4. 1539.
7. First and Second books of *Canzone villanesche a*3. 1541. (A. Einstein, *The Italian Madrigal*, Vol. III).
8. First book of madrigals *a*3. 1542.
9. First book of madrigals *a*4 *de diversi . . . autori a misura di breve*. 1542. (*Musica Divina*. 1583).
10. First book of madrigals *a*5. 1542. (*ibid*. 1563 ed.).
11. First book of *Canzone villanesche a*3. 1546. (As No. 7).
12. First book of madrigals *a*4. 1547.
13. Perissone – First book of madrigals *a*4. 1547. (As No. 9).
14. First book of madrigals *a*3. 1551. (*Opera Omnia*, ed. A. Main).
15. First book of madrigals *a*5. 1555. (*ibid*. 1557 ed.).
16. As No. 15. (As No. 15).
17. Fourth book of madrigals *a*5. 1557. (*ibid*. 1563 ed.).
18. Second book of madrigals *a*4. 1557. (*ibid*. 1571 ed.).
19. As No. 17. (As No. 17).
20. As No. 18. (As No. 18).
21. *Il secondo libro delle muse*. 1558. (First book of madrigals *a*4. 1583).
22. *Musica nova*. 1559.
23. *Il terzo libro delle muse*. 1561. (*Opera omnia* ed. R. Casimiri).
24. *Le vive fiamme*. 1565. (*Opera omnia* ed. B. Meier).
25. *Il desiderio secondo libro*. 1566. (As No. 9).
26. First book of madrigals *a*5. 1566. (As No. 7).
27. *Gli amorosi concenti*. 1568. (*Di Cipriano et Annibale madregali a quattro voci*. 1575).
28. First book of madrigals *a*4. 1568. (As No. 23).
29. First book of madrigals *a*6. 1569. (*ibid*, 1582 ed.).
30. Third book of madrigals *a*5. 1570. (As No. 9).
31. First book of *Giustiniane*. 1570. (*Journal of Renaissance and Baroque Music*, I, 1. ed. A. Einstein).
32. *Corona de madrigali*. 1579. (*Opera omnia* ed. A. Sandberger).
33. First book of madrigals *a*5. 1580.
34. Second book of madrigals *a*5. 1581.
35. Fourth book of madrigals *a*4. 1581. (*Opera omnia* ed. van den Borren).

36. First book of *Villanelle*. 1584.
37. Second book of *Canzonette*. 1584. (As No. 7).
38. Eighth book of madrigals a5. 1586.
39. As No. 38.
40. *Concerti* . . . 1587.
41. As No. 40.
42. Ninth book of madrigals a5. 1588. (*Opera omnia* ed. MacClintock).
43. Second book of madrigals a5. 1590. (*ibid.* 1607 ed.).
44. *Balletti* a5. 1591. (*ibid.* 1593 ed.).
45. As No. 44. (As No. 44).
46. Seventh book of madrigals a5. 1595.
47. Third book of madrigals a5. 1595. (*Opera omnia* ed. W. Weismann).
48. Fourth book of madrigals a5. 1596. (As No. 47).
49. *Canzonette* a3. 1597. (As No. 7).
50. Ninth book of madrigals a5. 1599.
51. Fourth book of madrigals a5. 1603.
52. As No. 51.
53. As No. 51.
54. Sixth book of madrigals a5. 1611. (As No. 47).
55. *Seconda scelta delli madrigali* a5. 1613. (As No. 7).

Acknowledgement
Alfred Einstein, *The Italian Madrigal*, trans. Alexander H. Krappe, Roger H.
Sessions, and Oliver Strunk. Copyright 1949, 1977 by Princeton University Press.
Excerpts reprinted by permission of Princeton University Press.

Translations

1. While sleeping one day at Baiae[1] in the shade lay Love,/ Where the murmuring of the springs pleased him more,/ The Nymphs ran to avenge his ardour/ And hid his lamp beneath the water,/ So that he would believe that within that liquid/ Suddenly an eternal fire was born;/ Whence at those baths always the heat lasts/ Because the flame of love heeds not water.

2. Love makes me die,/ And yet I wish to follow./ It is not a great grief that firmly and strongly/ I know that I go to my death./ Under a harsh fate/ I was born into the world to die I feel,/ And yet to embrace my torment pleases me./ Ah you who hear my deep lament/ Tell me I pray, if to speak is not distressing,/ 'Tis not a wonder this/ That Love makes me die,/ And yet I wish to follow.

3. My Italy, though words are no remedy/ For the mortal wounds/ That in your beautiful body I see so many,/ I would like at least my sighs to be such/ As the Tiber and the Arno hope for,/ and the Po, where sorrowful and sad I now sit./ Ruler of heaven, I ask/ That the pity that led you to earth/ May turn you towards your beloved divine country:/ See, noble Lord,/ From what trivial causes arises such a cruel war;/ And the hearts, hardened and closed/ By Mars proud and fierce/ Do you open, Father, and soften and free;/ There make your truth,/ However unworthy I may be, through my tongue be heard.

4. The more the fire burns me and sets me alight,/ Lady, for you, the more love pleases me,/ Nor for me is the sadness pain/ For sweet it is to me to die, the distress a game./ It is not icy my ice,/ Neither does my flame torment/ Nor the pain sadden nor death kill me,/ So gentle is the bond/ And so sweet my hurt/ That it distresses not my life, but rather smiles upon it,/ Wherefore neither do I beg Love to challenge me,/ But to freeze, enflame, kill and clasp me,/ And in my heart to depict/ True faith, true love and sweet fire.

5. So sweet is the fire and so gentle the knot/ With which you enflame me, love, with which you bind me,/ That being burnt and caught I enjoy;/ Nor shall I try ever to extinguish or untie/ The fire or the noose; indeed I wish that always/ Will languish my heart in such a sweet condition.

6. The white and gentle swan dies singing, and I/ Weeping reach the end of my life./ What strange and diverse fate that he dies unconsoled,/ And I die blessed./ Death, which in dying/ Fills me full of joy and desire./ If in dying no other pain I feel/ With a thousand deaths a day I would be content.

---

1. A hot springs resort, popular in Roman times.

7. (i) Who the galliard, lady, wishes to learn,/ Come to us who are fine teachers,/ For at night and in the morning we never fail to play; Tantantan tarira rarirura.
(ii) Try and see, you will want to call us/ After we have been up ten times,/ For at night (*etc.*)
(iii) Who the galliard, lady, wishes to learn/ Has to be under the master,/ For at night (*etc.*)
(iv) And to her who is a beginner I want to give/ This partner whose name is Martino,/ For at night (*etc.*)

8. (See No. 1).

9. I am a young lady, and gladly/ Rejoice and sing in the new season,/ Thanks to love and to my sweet thoughts./ I go through green meadows looking/ At the white flowers, the yellow and red,/ the roses above their thorns, and white lilies,/ And all of these I go on comparing/ To the face of him in whose love/ I was taken and will be held forever.

10. Strange cliffs, harsh mountains, heights trembling,/ Ruins and stones to the sky naked and bare,/ Where with great difficulty can ascend such steep/ Clouds in this steamy smoky air;/ Magnificent horror, silent woods and so many/ Black grassy caves amid broken stones open;/ Abandoned barren deserts,/ Where fear to go the wild beasts wandering./ In the guise of a man by excessive pain/ His sad heart afflicted, beside himself,/ Wanders weeping, where his madness takes him,/ Weeping go I amongst you, and if this course of action/ Changes not the sky, with voice more full/ I shall beyond the melancholy shadows be heard.

11. (i) All old hags are malicious,/ For they have lost their true season:/ This I say to you, old schemer.
(ii) Arrogant, ingrate, wretched and foul;/ And who does not believe it, look at their faces./ This I say (*etc.*)
(iii) The best of them are all wheezing,/ What else do they but cough at night?/ This I say (*etc.*)
(iv) Flee all these bitter old hags,/ O girls who have to find a husband,/ Be at your pleasure, let them burst.

12. I was weaving these leaves and those/ For my good Daphne to wear on her head./ But behold, a sudden horrible storm,/ And my little garlands/ And my beautiful leaves/ And the plants and the bank and the stream, it took them away./ Who will comfort, alas, who will console me?

13. Although when I depart/ I feel myself dying,/ To part I would like always, at every moment,/ So great is the pleasure that I feel/ From the life I gain on coming back./ And thus thousands of times a day/ To part from you I would like,/ So sweet is my returning.

14. O most unjust Love, why so rarely/ Do you make harmonious our desires?/ Wherefore, treacherous one, is it that to you is so dear/ The discordant desire that within two hearts you see?/ You let me not wander to the easy and clear ford,/ And into the darkest depths you drag me:/ From she who desires my love you recall me,/ And she who hates me you wish that I adore and love.

15. My kind fortune and happy life,/ The clear days and peaceful nights/ And gentle sighs, and the sweet style/ That used to resound in verses and in rhymes,/

Turned suddenly to sorrow and to weeping,/ To hate life make me, and long for death./ Cruel, bitter, inexorable Death,/ You give me cause never to be happy,/ But to pass all my life in weeping,/ The days dark and sorrowful the nights;/ My deep sighs go not in rhymes,/ And my harsh fate conquers all styles.

16. I sang, now I weep; and no less of sweetness/ From weeping do I take than from singing I took,/ Since to the cause, not to the effect, intent/ Are my senses desirous of nobility:/ Thence gentleness and harshness/ And actions proud and humble and courteous/ I endure equally; neither do burdens weigh me down,/ nor is my armour by a little scorn shattered./ So let them keep towards me their usual style,/ Love, my lady, the world and my fortune;/ For I do not think that I shall be anything but happy./ Be it living, or dying, or languishing, a more noble/ State than mine there is not under the moon,/ So sweet is the root of my bitterness.

17. O death, eternal end of all misfortunes,/ Repose of body and of mind,/ Useful and necessary to animals/ Much more than life if one thinks well on it;/ Haven for the blind and miserable mortals/ Who wandering go from east to west:/ You prisons destroy and break harsh chains,/ And put an end to amorous pains.

18. O sleep, O the quiet, damp and shadowy/ Night's peaceful child, O of mortals/ Afflicted the comfort, oblivion sweet of ills/ So grave, whence is life harsh and tedious,/ Help my heart that now is waning and rest/ Has not, and these limbs, weary and frail,/ Lift up. Envelop me, O sleep, and your wings/ Dark over me spread and place./ Where is the silence which the day flees and the light,/ And the gentle dreams which with no certain/ Trace attend you usually?/ Alas in vain I call you, and these gloomy and/ Icy shadows in vain I entice: O plumes/ With harshness filled, O nights painful and hard.

19. The noble lord, before whom it is of no avail/ To hide or flee or defend oneself,/ With sweet pleasure has my mind kindled/ With a burning and amorous arrow;/ And although the first blow harsh and fatal/ Was by itself, to complete his undertaking/ An arrow of pity he has taken/ And from both sides my heart pierces and assails./ One wound burns and pours forth fire and flame,/ The other tears, which the pain distills,/ Through my eyes, for your cruel condition;/ Nor, by means of the two fountains, does a single spark/ Lessen the fire that inflames me;/ On the contrary through pity increases my desire.

20. (See No. 15).

21. Who will ascend for me, my Lady, to heaven/ To bring back my lost reason/ Which, since departed from your beautiful eyes the dart/ That my heart pierced, every hour I am losing?/ Nor of such a loss do I complain,/ Provided it increases not, but remains at this degree;/ For I doubt, if more it diminishes,/ That foolish I shall go through the world wandering.

22. (See No. 16).

23. I am wounded, alas! And who gave it me/ To accuse I would, but have no proof;/ And without proof suspicion of evil is not believed:/ Nor spouts blood my strange wound./ I suffer agony and die; the cut is not seen./ My enemy is armed again./ To return to her will be a cruel predicament,/ For only she can cure me who wounded me.

24. This my exhausted and sorrowful heart/ With grief overflows, since with me it feels/ That shortly shall our sweetnesses be extinguished,/ Wherefore I must pass in weeping the hours./ It could be that my deep sorrow/ In departing from my sun is not powerful enough/ To send my soul to where she to wander consents,/ For then of her nest it shall remain outside./ O happy days of mine fleeting and brief,/ How quickly you disappear and lead me/ Into those most unhappy, sorrowful and dark./ Ah you who my life today uplifts,/ May you in your desires, angry stars/ And ungrateful cruel skies, never ever find.

25. Clothed the hills and the countryside around/ Did Spring with fresh glories,/ And breathed sweet Arabian fragrances,/ Girded with grasses and with flowers her tresses adorned./ When Licoris at the appearance of day,/ Gathering in his hand purple flowers,/ Said to me: 'In recompense of so much ardour/ For you I gather them, and behold I you with them adorn.'/ Thus my hair, sweetly/ Speaking, he girded,/ And in such gentle bands he enfolded/ My heart, that other pleasure it feels not./ Thus shall it never be that no more I love him,/ He of my eyes, nor shall it be that my mind/ For others sigh, or longingly call.

26. Two fresh roses gathered in paradise/ The other day bloomed the first of May,/ A fair gift from a lover old and wise/ Between two young lovers equally divided,/ With such sweet words and with a smile/ That would enamour even a wild man,/ Through a bright and amorous ray/ Caused the one and the other to change their countenance./ 'Such a pair of lovers the sun will never see,'/ He said, laughing while he sighed,/ And holding both, he turned around./ Thus he divided the roses and the words,/ So that even now my heart is glad and fears./ O happy eloquence, O joyful day!

27. In the air this day I have built so strong/ A castle that Jove to strike it down could not,/ Built upon two inconstant wheels,/ Of dust and wind are the doors,/ With a thousand ditches around, and its guards/ Are vain hopes, of every effect empty./ Of desire are the walls, where beats/ Not the sea, nor river, but tempests and destiny./ Of foolish daring and of fear are made/ The arms, which against another to fight know not how,/ And of various thoughts the ammunition./ Against himself the castellan fights,/ Paying his warriors only with ambition:/ Think of my deeds, for they the end shall be.

28. Towards dawn, when so gently the breeze/ In Spring is wont to move the flowers/ And the little birds begin their songs/ So sweetly, the thoughts within my soul/ Move me I feel towards she who has them all in her power,/ That to return I needs must to my music.

29. Graceful nymphs and tiny cupids,/ Who amid the hills of Mars hide yourselves,/ To my happiness joyfully run/ Strewing roses and fragrant flowers;/ White swans and you wise shepherds/ At the sound of the song your souls kindle,/ To Venus, to Love with me pay/ For such beautiful graces eternal honour./ The sweet and desired fruit I have gathered,/ I have even that pretty sun held in my arms,/ Which with its great heat makes bloom the roses;/ So great is the contentment where I am buried/ And the joys that I have in my breast hidden/ That I from myself alone delight in loving and am silent.

30. Ah, who disturbs my sleep, ah, who deprives me,/ Miserable, of that good which all other surpasses?/ Who takes from my hand that hope/ Which had already, weary, once been led to the shore?/ With me was my lady now when I

slept,/ And so sweet appeared to me her countenance,/ That with her to speak I was emboldened,/ My closest thoughts wholly to her I opened./ At which she, moved: 'In recompense of this/ Your faith, as reward for so much love,/ Here I am', she said, 'obedient to your wishes.'/ Ah, that while I embrace her and full of passion/ Clasp her, jealous, the sun swiftly awakens me,/ Which, wounding my eyes, killed my heart.

31. (i) When will that day ever come/ When these girls will make love to us?/ Would you like us to dance around/ With our trousers down?
(ii) O what delicate flesh,/ Have a look, dear cousin,/ For one has not the appetite/ Such as the heart would like.
(iii) Look awhile at that pretty little face,/ Because when we look at it/ It makes all in flames/ Our belly and intestines.
(iv) Maidens of pearls and of velvet,/ Maidens of gems and of scarlet,/ With what strong and powerful pain/ You have stolen our hearts indeed.
(v) You are beautiful and well-formed,/ And we are three old men./ If you want good company,/ We would give you little spigots.

32. So that I may escape alive from these hazardous rocks/ And reach my exile a beautiful conclusion,/ How I long to turn the sail/ And drop anchor in some port!/ Except that I burn like kindled wood,/ So hard it is for me to leave my accustomed life./ Lord of my end and of my life,/ Before I break the ship among the rocks,/ Direct to a good port my tired sail.

33. What doth today my sun,/ What doth my song and music,/ If they sing not of her glory and her name?/ Now these my violets/ And these flowers to her I give/ That she may make of them a crown for her tresses.

34. Now returns to brighten the air and the earth/ Young April, laden with flowers;/ The sea becomes calm, the frost flies underground,/ Frolic the pretty nymphs and their shepherds./ Return the birds to amorous war,/ Happy to sing in the morning dawn./ And I mourn the night and am sorrowful/ As soon as the sun reveals itself in the east.

35. Let me see again, after so much war,/ Of peace a shadow, and after so much scorn,/ A happy glance, whence unlocks/ Love his rays, while one perceives, surrounding/ That lady, pity that can the earth/ Cover with roses and make the night day./ May brief joy temper long suffering/ With the respite of two most brief hours.

36. (i) I shall flee so much, Love,/ That it will lessen the passion,/ The flames and the chains/ Which hold this soul in so much pain.
(ii) I shall flee so much, so much,/ That cease will my weeping,/ The knot, the bow, and the arrow,/ Which hold this soul in grief bitter and mortal.
(iii) I shall flee the powerful bond,/ And shall escape the snare,/ Nor of fleeing do I repent,/ And of lessening this passion which in my heart I feel.
(iv) I shall flee therefore Love,/ Released from the raging passion,/ And I shall say in fleeing:/ 'Lady you are the reason for my torment.'

37. While the cuckoo his cuckoo was singing,/ 'Leave,' Amaryllis was saying,/ 'Leave Damon your Phyllis,/ And run into my arms, run my heart./ Cuckoo, cuckoo, do you not hear?/ He you invites and I.'

38. Pretty birds amid the green fronds/ Harmonize in competition their wanton little notes;/ Murmurs the breeze, and makes the leaves and waves/ Flutter, as variously she strikes them./ When silent are the birds loudly she replies;/ When sing the birds, more softly she shakes;/ Be it by chance or art, now she accompanies and now/ Alternates their verses with her musical breeze.

39. Forsennata cried out: 'O you who take/ With you part of me, and part you leave,/ O take one or give back the other, or death/ Give together to both: halt, halt your steps,/ Only so that to you may my last words be carried;/ I say not kisses: another more worthy shall have/ Those from you. What fear you, cruel, if you stay?/ You can refuse, since to flee you are able.'

40. I go weeping for times past,/ Which I spent loving a mortal thing/ Without raising myself in flight, though possessing wings/ To make, perhaps, of myself not a base example./ You who see my wrongdoing unworthy and wicked,/ King of Heaven, invisible, immortal,/ Give aid to my soul led astray and frail,/ And her lack with your grace make good;/ So that, if I have lived in war and tempest,/ I may die in peace and in port; and if my sojourn/ Was devoted to vanity, at least may my departure be honest./ To what little life that to me remains/ And to my death deign to be at hand:/ You know well that in others I have no hope.

41. Thyrsis to die desired,/ In the eyes gazing of her whom he adored,/ When she, who of him no less was fired,/ To him said: 'Alas my love,/ Ah die not yet,/ With you I desire to die also.'/ Restrained Thyrsis the desire/ That he had for his life to end,/ Though feeling death, he could not die,/ And while his look steadily he held/ On her lovely eyes divine,/ And amorous nectar from them drank,/ His lovely nymph, that already was nigh/ To feeling the fruits of Love,/ Said, with eyes languid and trembling:/ 'Die, my heart, for I die.'/ To whom replied the shepherd:/ 'And I, my life, die.'/ Thus died the fortunate lovers/ Of death so sweet and so pleasant,/ That again to die they returned to life.

42. (See No. 15).

43. Lo murmur the waves/ And tremble the fronds/ In the breeze of dawn, and the young trees,/ And upon the green branches the pretty birds/ Sing sweetly,/ And laughs the East./ Lo already the dawn appears/ And is reflected in the sea/ And clears the sky/ And makes pearly the delicate ice/ And the high mountains gilds./ O beautiful and fair dawn,/ The breeze is your messenger, and your breeze/ Every inflamed heart restores.

44. *The Prize-winner*
(i) Where are you going in such haste,/ O vital spirit of my heart?/ Fa la./ Far from you, my goddess,/ How do you wish that I live?/ Fa la./ Either you here remain or let me come,/ For without you I needs must die./ Fa la.
(ii) From a thousand nymphs Love/ Has you for me alone chosen./ Fa la./ Ah change into happiness/ The soul that to weeping is accustomed./ Fa la./ May Amaryllis cease to be cruel,/ For you know well how faithful I am to you./ Fa la./
(iii) O may you be blessed/ Since you depart not yet./ Fa la./ May now flee from me every worry,/ Happy let us live in joy./ Fa la./ Let us jest, let us kiss, O my shining sun,/ Nature and Love thus commands and wishes./ Fa la.
(iv) Perfect joy such as I feel/ No other shepherd feels./ Fa la./ Your arrows, and the fire,/ You have turned, Love, into a game./ Fa la./ And your reward, O powerful winged Archer,/ I now enjoy, the crown of your every pleasure./ Fa la.

45. *Good spirits*
(i) To live happily I wish/ Without any deep sorrow./ La la./ You can cease, Love,/ From shooting my heart;/ Make use of your sharp arrows/ Where they may not seem weak;/ I have little or no esteem for you/ And I make fun of you./ La la.
(ii) Without any thought/ I enjoy real pleasure./ La la./ Neither can you with your torments/ Trouble my rejoicing;/ Put out your light/ For it neither burns nor destroys me,/ I fear not your fire/ And I make fun of you./ La la.
(iii) Bacchus I adore and love/ And I yearn for his liquor./ La la./ And he makes me happy/ And is to me dear delight;/ With him both night and day/ I willingly stay,/ To him always happily I call,/ And I make fun of you./ La la.

46. Cruel Amaryllis, who with your name still/ To love, ah wearily, bitterly, you teach;/ Amaryllis than the white privet/ More white and more beautiful,/ But than the deaf snake/ More deaf and more wild and more fleeting;/ Since that to speak I offend you/ I shall die in silence./ But shall shout for me the shores and mountains/ And this wood to whom/ So often your fair name/ To echo I have taught;/ For me the weeping springs/ And murmuring winds/ Shall speak of my laments;/ Shall be declared in my face/ The pity and the pain,/ And if is silent every other thing at the end/ My dying shall speak,/ And my death will tell you of my torment.

47. I languish and die, ah, cruel one!/ But you, savage cause of my fate,/ Ah, for pity's sake, comfort/ So painful a death/ With a single tear,/ Whence may be said at the end of my languishing:/ 'Now that you be merciful, sweet it is to die.'

48. Eyes serene and clear/ You burn me, yet feels my heart/ In the burning delight, not pain./ Sweet words and dear/ You wound me, yet feels my breast/ Not pain in the wound, but delight./ O miracle of love!/ A soul that is all afire and all bleeding/ Is consumed and grieves not, dies and languishes not.

49. (i) A shepherd the other day,/ Looking as if he was of life deprived,/ Languishing, was heard to say: 'I am wounded, alas[1].'
(ii) To him I went near,/ Who was motionless as a stone,/ And he said only: 'I am wounded, alas.'
(iii) 'Quiet', I said, 'shepherd,/ For the wound is slight, have no doubt,/ For the wounder yet can heal you.'
(iv) 'And who is this physician/ Who can heal my heart from the harsh passing?' 'Livia, if she sings: "I am wounded, alas".'
(v) 'Then gentle Livia,/ Sing, sing, and to death no more shall I pass,/ And life shall be mine: "I am wounded, alas".'

50. Alone and pensive the most deserted fields/ I go measuring with steps dragging and slow,/ And my eyes intently watch in order to flee/ From where any trace of man the sand imprints./ No other defence do I find that saves me/ From the plain knowledge of people,/ Because in my actions, of joy devoid,/ From without one may read how within I blaze;/ So that I believe now that mountains and shores/ And rivers and woods know the temper/ Of my life, which is hidden from others./ But still such harsh paths nor so wild/ To seek I know not, that Love comes not always/ Discoursing with me, and I with him.

51. I wish to die/ Now that I kiss, love,/ The beautiful mouth of my beloved heart./ Ah dear and sweet tongue,/ Give me so much spirit/ That with sweetness in this

---

1. The music to this phrase quotes the opening of Palestrina's madrigal (see No. 23).

breast it may extinguish/ Alas my life. To this white breast/ Ah clasp me until I swoon./ Ah mouth, ah kisses, ah tongue, again I say/ I wish to die.

52. Ah painful parting,/ Ah end of my life,/ From you I part and die not?/ And yet I feel the pain of death,/ And sense in parting/ A living death/ Which gives life to the pain/ That kills for ever my heart.

53. That little bird that sings/ So sweetly and wantonly flies/ Now from the fir tree to the beech/ And now from the beech to the myrtle,/ If he had human spirit/ He would say I burn with love,/ But so well burns he in his heart/ And calls his desire/ That I respond I burn of love also./ May you be blessed,/ Loving, gentle, pretty little bird.

54. Cease troubling me,/ Thought cruel and vain,/ For it can never be that which pleases you!/ Death is for me a joy,/ Wherein it is not permitted to hope/ To be happier.

55. Go my laments/ Hastily in flight/ To her who is the cause of my eternal sorrow;/ Tell her for pity's sake to be to me/ Sweetly cruel,/ Not cruelly adverse,/ Then my doleful cries/ I shall change happily into loving cries.